# Words from Other Languages

by Jody Jackson

Editorial Offices: Glenview, Illinois • Parsippany, New Jersey • New York, New York
Sales Offices: Needham, Massachusetts • Duluth, Georgia • Glenview, Illinois
Coppell, Texas • Sacramento, California • Mesa, Arizona

All languages change as time passes. The English language has added many new words during hundreds of years. Some words are "borrowed" from other languages.

For example, have you ever seen a chipmunk? When English-speaking settlers came to America, they didn't have a name for this little animal. They learned a Native American name, *atchitamon.* Over time, this became the word *chipmunk* in English.

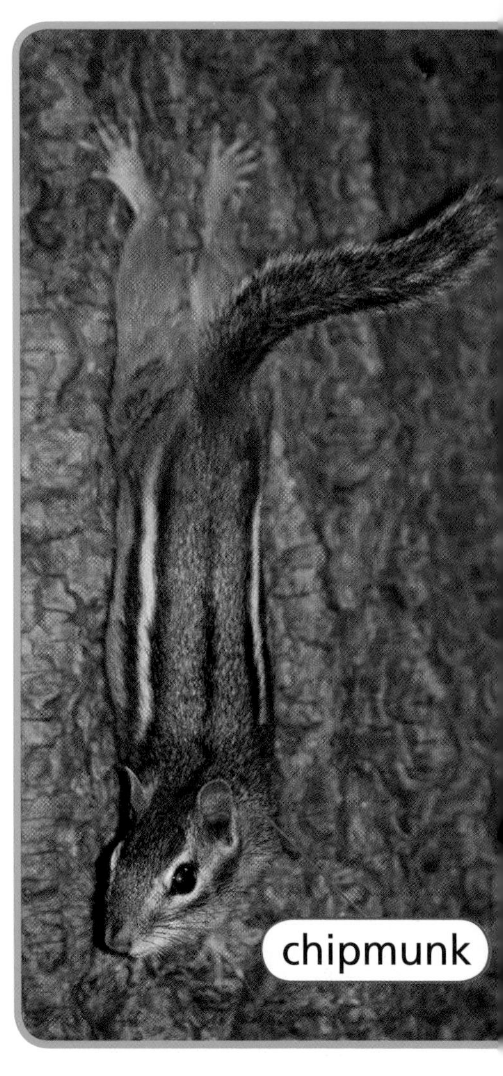


*Chipmunk* comes from an Ojibwa word that means "head-first." When a chipmunk comes down from a tree, its head points to the ground.

*Skunk* comes from an Abenaki word that means "one who squirts, or sprays."

The English-speaking settlers didn't have words for many new things in America. So they began to use some Native American words. Over time, the words changed as they became popular in the English language.

Today, English is the most common language in the United States. But many other languages are spoken here. Sometimes words from those languages become part of the English language. Let's look at some examples.

## *In the Kitchen*

Some food names come from other languages. Have you ever eaten yams? The word *yam* comes from *nyami,* a West African word that means "to eat."

Yams come from Africa.

Do you ever cook a meal outdoors? A meal cooked outside can be called a *barbecue*. This word probably comes from the Arawak Indians of Haiti. Long ago, the Arawak people would cook food over a fire, using a frame of sticks called a *barbakoa.*

Today people often use a barbecue to cook food outside.

## *In Your Closet*

Do you have clothes made of denim? Blue jeans are made of denim. The word *denim* comes from a city in France called *Nîmes.* The French word *de* can mean "from." So *denim* means "cloth from Nîmes."

Do you put on pajamas before going to bed? The word *pajamas* came to English from India. The word *pajamas* comes from Persian, or Iranian, words. Pajamas, and their name, came to America from Europeans who had lived in India.

The word *pajamas* comes from two Persian words: *pae,* which means "leg," and *jamah,* which means "clothing."

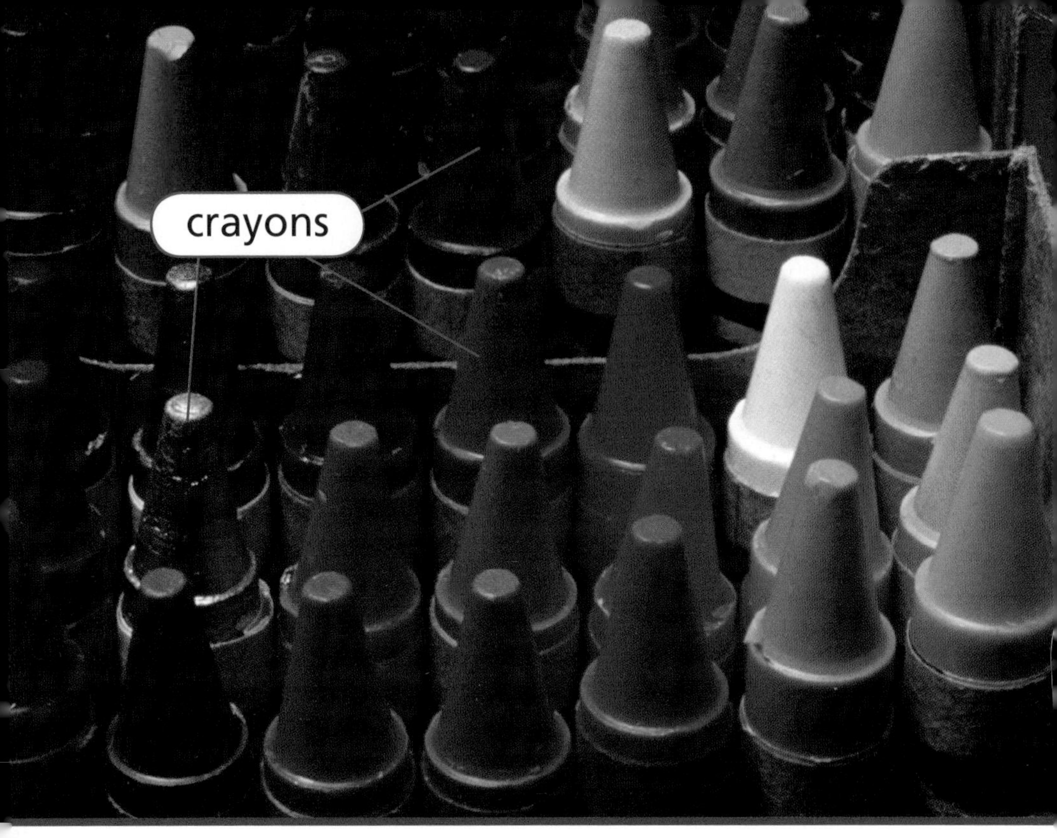


Did you ever use a crayon to write on paper?

## *In School*

In school, you might use crayons. *Crayon* is a French word. But in French, *crayon* means "pencil."

The word *paper* has gone through many changes. The ancient Egyptians made a kind of paper from the papyrus plant. Ancient Romans, who spoke Latin, named paper *papyrus.* The French borrowed the word and changed it to *papier.* The English borrowed this word, changed it to *papir*, and finally to *paper,* the word we use today.

## *At the Zoo*

Zoo animals come from all over the world. So do their names.

Kangaroos come from Australia. Their name probably comes from the Aborigines. Aborigines are native people of Australia.

The word *alligator* probably comes from the Spanish word for lizard, *el lagarto.*

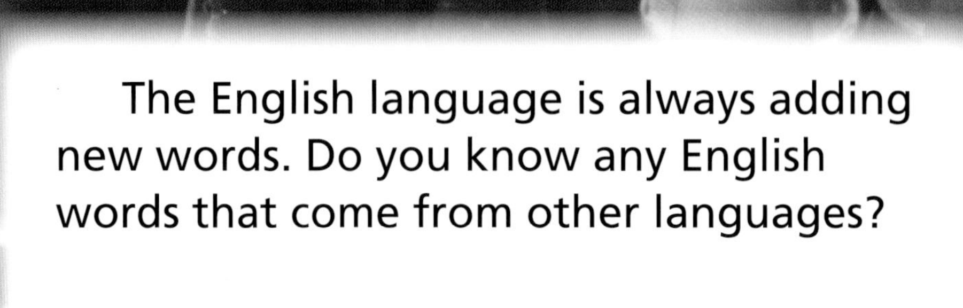

The English language is always adding new words. Do you know any English words that come from other languages?

## *Index*

This index tells where to find information about the words mentioned in this book.